Disguises, Explosions, & Boiling Farts

Bizarre Insect Defenses

by Ruth Owen and Ross Piper

Ruby Tuesday Books

Published in 2018 by Ruby Tuesday Books Ltd.

Editor: Mark J. Sachner
Designer: Emma Randall
Production: John Lingham

Photo credits
Alamy: 24, 27 (bottom center), 28 (bottom), 29 (bottom left); Creative Commons: 15 (bottom), 25 (top); FLPA: 4, 9 (bottom), 14, 16, 20, 27 (bottom left); Getty Images: 19 (top), 25 (bottom); Istock Photo: 6 (bottom); Nature Picture Library: 5 (center), 6–7, 10, 15 (top); Ross Piper: 12 (center), 13 (bottom); Ruby Tuesday Books: 12 (bottom); Shutterstock: Cover, 1, 5 (top), 5 (bottom), 7 (center), 8, 11, 13 (top), 17, 18, 19 (bottom), 21, 22–23, 26, 27 (top), 27 (bottom right), 28 (top), 29 (top), 29 (center), 29 (bottom right), 31.

Library of Congress Control Number: 2017918124

Print ISBN 978-1-78856-010-8
eBook ISBN 978-1-78856-011-5

Printed and published in the United States of America

For further information including rights and permissions requests, please contact our Customer Service Department at 877-337-8577.

Words shown in **bold** in the text are explained in the glossary

Contents

Masters of Defense

Maybe you're fat and juicy. Perhaps you're shiny and crunchy. One thing is for sure—you're bite-sized!

Life as a tiny insect means you're in constant danger of becoming another animal's meal. That's why insects have developed a whole bunch of ways to stay safe—from fighting back and high-speed escapes, to hiding and disguises.

Inside this book, we'll see up-close how some of Earth's tiniest creatures stay safe from **predators**.

Let's discover the secret world of insect defenses. . . .

Now You See Me, Now You Don't!

The quartz grasshopper in this photo is hard to spot among the rocks and pebbles of its desert home.

Packed with Poison

The dogbane leaf beetle feeds on poisonous plants such as milkweed and dogbane. The insect stores the plant's poisons inside its body, making itself **toxic** to predators. The beetle's colorful, shiny body warns its enemies that it's not good to eat.

A dogbane leaf beetle

POISON

A lichen katydid

Lichen

A Master of Disguise

The dark body of this **lichen** katydid is decorated with pale silvery-green lines. The pattern allows the insect to easily blend in among the fluffy tufts of real lichen on a branch.

The Science Stuff—What Is an Insect?

- Insects are tiny animals with a body made of three main parts.

- Insects use their **antennae** to do different things, such as touching, smelling, or detecting sounds.

- An insect has a tough outer covering called an **exoskeleton**.

Antennae

The head contains an insect's brain, eyes, mouthparts, and a pair of antennae.

The **thorax** has six jointed legs and the insect's wings.

The **abdomen** contains an insect's digestive system and reproductive parts.

Take Aim, Fire!

It's early morning in a forest. Thousands of wood ants are scurrying from their nest.

The ants are leaving their home to **forage** for food. Suddenly, a large, dark, fast-moving shape blocks out the sun. A hungry bird has spotted the ant nest and is swooping down toward the tiny insects.

The ants instantly defend themselves. They spray stinky jets of a chemical called formic acid into the air. Startled by the attack, the bird changes its mind and flies off to find its breakfast elsewhere!

Wood ants spraying formic acid

A wood ant sprays acid from its abdomen.

A drop of acid

Abdomen

Formic acid gets its name from the word *formica*, which means "ant" in Latin.

The Science Stuff

Some birds deliberately land on ants and annoy them in order to get sprayed with acid. Why?

Scientists don't know for sure—yet. One theory is that the acid kills **mites** or lice on a bird's body and feathers. The birds may be using the ants' acid to keep healthy and kill off pests.

Ant Acid for Hunting

When an ant captures another insect, worm, or slug, it grips its **prey** with its jaws and front legs. Then the ant sprays formic acid onto its victim to kill it. Once the creature stops struggling, the ant carries its meal back to the nest.

Worm

Wood ants

Large prey, such as a worm, will be captured and transported home by a team of ants.

A Very Sticky End

Hungry predators aren't the only dangers faced by ants. An ant **colony** must also defend its **territory** from invasion by rival ants.

In the forests of Malaysia, one type of carpenter ant takes defending its nest and food supply to an extreme and explosive level.

When faced with an invading ant, the carpenter ant grabs its enemy with its jaws and legs. Then the carpenter ant explodes. It sprays the invader with a thick, yellow gloop made up of poison and glue. Both ants are instantly killed—attacker and defender!

The Science Stuff

Most ants have **glands** in their heads that contain chemicals used for sending messages to other ants. Inside an exploding ant, these glands spread from the head into the thorax and abdomen.

The glands are filled with the poisonous yellow gloop.

When it's under attack, an exploding ant bends and squeezes its abdomen. It forces its glands and body to **rupture**, blasting thick, toxic glue all over its enemy.

Exploding carpenter ant

Gland filled with attack gloop

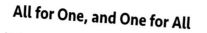
All for One, and One for All
Why would a carpenter ant sacrifice its life by blowing itself up? Ants are social insects. This means they live in huge groups, sharing the work of protecting their queen, raising young, defending the nest, and finding food. The survival of the colony is more important than the life of a single ant.

The corpses of this carpenter ant and her much larger attacker are glued together in a sticky death grip.

Attacking ant

Carpenter ant

Butts of Fire

Ok. So everybody does it. But the tiny bombardier beetle takes farting to a whole new level.

These little guys can unleash an explosive, scorching blast of burning chemicals from their butts. Why do they do this?

Birds, frogs, spiders, and other insects all eat beetles. A bombardier beetle's superheated, stinging butt attack is its defense mechanism. Any predator that gets too close will soon regret its choice of snack as it's sprayed over and over with noxious burning chemicals.

Take that, giant finger monster!

The blast reaches a temperature of 212°F (100°C).

The beetle can release up to 500 farts in a second!

The jet of chemicals can travel more than 12 inches (30 cm).

The Science Stuff

1. Inside a bombardier beetle's abdomen are glands that produce chemicals called hydrogen peroxide and hydroquinones.

2. The chemicals are stored in a reservoir, or storage chamber.

3. When the beetle is under attack, the reservoir empties into the reaction chamber. The reaction chamber contains substances that instantly turn the chemicals into an explosive mixture of high-pressure gas, boiling water, and stinging chemicals.

4. BOOM! The mixture is expelled as a jet. The jet isn't a true fart as it doesn't come from the beetle's digestive system. But it's hot and stinky, and has enemies running for cover!

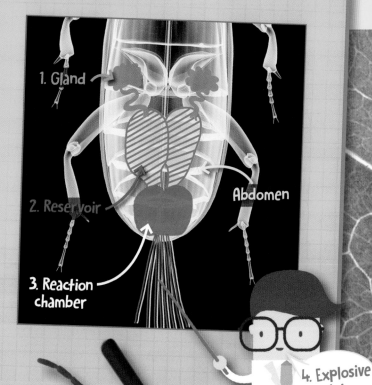

1. Gland

2. Reservoir

Abdomen

3. Reaction chamber

4. Explosive jet

How Come the Beetle Doesn't Explode?

The walls of the reaction chamber are so tough they can withstand the explosive chemical reaction. Also (thankfully for the beetle), the explosion instantly leaves its butt.

Take Aim, Fire!

Some bombardier beetles can aim their farts with devastating precision. They can fire to the left, to the right, over their heads, and even under their own bodies through their legs!

High-precision butt

11

A Butt-Propelled Getaway

When it's in danger, the tiny stenus rove beetle makes a high-speed, jet-propelled getaway. It does this by squirting a chemical called stenusin from its butt!

Imagine the scene. . . . The beetle is hunting on the edge of a pond. Suddenly it spots a frog. To escape from this huge predator, the beetle scurries out onto the pond—walking on water.

This stenus rove beetle is about the size of a grain of rice.

Next, it quickly squirts stenusin onto the water. As the chemical hits the pond's surface, everything floating nearby is blasted away from the chemical—including the beetle. Steering with its butt, the beetle zooms across the water's surface, and away from danger!

To Infinity and Beyond!

The speed at which the tiny beetle is propelled across the pond is like you traveling at up to 500 miles per hour (800 km/h)!

The Science Stuff

Test out the beetle's speedy getaway for yourself.

You will need:

- A mixing bowl of water
- Ground pepper
- Liquid dishwashing detergent

1 Sprinkle pepper over the surface of the water.

2 Squirt a drop of detergent into the water.

3 The pepper grains will hurtle across the water's surface away from the detergent. Why does this happen?

Water molecules stick tightly together on the surface of water, creating a skin-like effect called surface tension. Pepper grains float on water because they are not heavy enough to break the surface tension.

Once the detergent touches the water, it breaks the surface tension. However, the water molecules still try to stick together. They instantly move away from the detergent, carrying the pepper grains with them.

A tiny, light rove beetle is able to walk on water without breaking the surface tension. Once it squirts stenusin into the water, however, the chemical breaks the water's surface tension, just like detergent. The beetle is whizzed across the water as the fast-moving water molecules try to get away from the chemical.

Grabbing a Snack

One of the beetle's mouthparts is called the labium. This telescopic mouthpart shoots out to grab teeny, tiny insects and other prey.

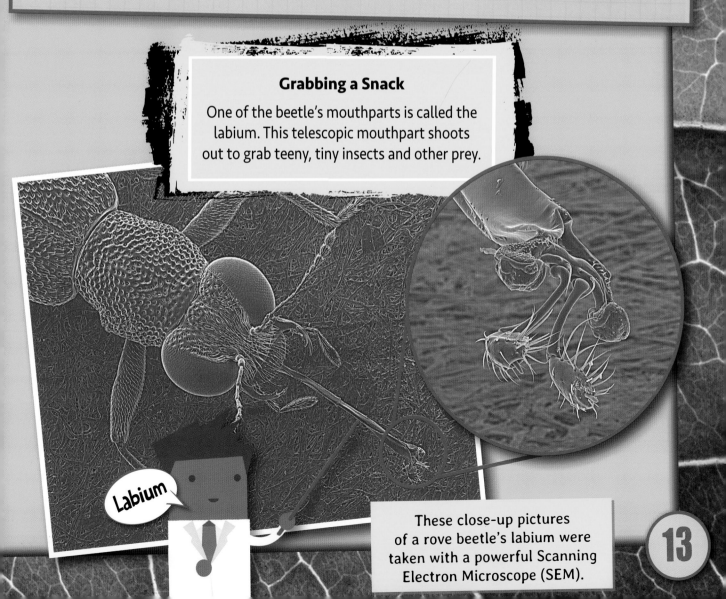

Labium

These close-up pictures of a rove beetle's labium were taken with a powerful Scanning Electron Microscope (SEM).

13

A Night-Time Battle

In the Arizona desert, a nightly battle takes place between bats and moths.

Bats hunt for moths and other flying insects using a system called **echolocation**. As a bat flies through the darkness, it makes **ultrasonic** sounds. These waves of sound bounce off an insect and return to the bat.

The bat uses the sound waves to create a picture of the world around it. The sound waves tell the bat where its prey is located and how far away. Then the bat gives chase!

How echolocation works:
- Bat sound waves
- Returning sound waves

A tiger moth

Tiger moths have developed a way to block a bat's echolocation system. When it senses a bat, the moth makes its own clicking sounds. The clicks interfere with the bat's noises and make it impossible for the bat to locate its prey.

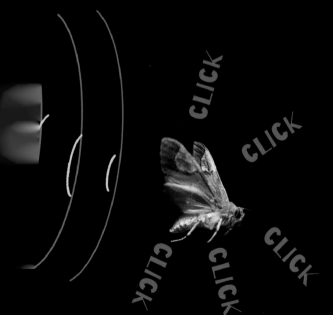

CLICK CLICK CLICK CLICK CLICK

Confusing the Enemy!

To block a bat's echolocation system, a tiger moth makes up to 4,500 clicking sounds per second!

Warning Signs and Deadly Bubbles

The koppie foam grasshopper from Africa is exactly what its name says. It's a grasshopper that produces foam. Poisonous foam!

This insect has a two-part strategy to keep it safe. First, it has red, blue, or yellow patterns on its exoskeleton. These bright colors are a warning label that tells predators, "I am poisonous. Do not eat me!"

If a hungry attacker decides to risk it and grabs the grasshopper, the insect releases a highly toxic foam from glands in its thorax. The foam tastes so disgusting the attacker gives up and may even become very sick.

Koppie foam grasshopper

As the foam is released from the grasshopper's body, it makes a scary, hissing noise.

The foam is so stinky it can scare predators away.

Poisonous Foam

A Deadly Snack

The koppie foam grasshopper's whole body is poisonous, not just the foam. If a predator dares to eat this insect, it could be killed. The poison is powerful enough to kill an animal the size of a dog!

A koppie foam grasshopper is about 3 inches (7.5 cm) long.

The Science Stuff

Why is the foaming grasshopper so poisonous?

Foaming grasshoppers feed on poisonous plants, such as milkweeds.

The poisons are stored in the grasshopper's body, but they don't harm the insect.

The grasshopper's foam is actually the insect's poisonous blood filled with air bubbles to make it frothy.

Milkweed

Spiny and Dangerous

If a hungry predator decides to snack on a cup moth caterpillar, it will receive a nasty sting!

These caterpillars have hundreds of spines on their bodies. Each spine is a hollow tube filled with **venom**. If a predator gets too close, the spines pierce the attacker's flesh. The tips of the spines break off, and stinging venom is injected into the predator's skin.

To warn potential attackers that it's armed and dangerous, a cup moth caterpillar's body is often decorated with brightly colored dots and patterns.

Cup moth caterpillar

Spines

The venom is produced by a gland at the base of each spine.

If you touch the spines of a cup moth caterpillar, its sting feels like a stinging nettle.

Some of the caterpillar's spines grow from parts called tubercles.

Tubercle

18

Cocoon

A moth emerging from its cocoon

Cap

Adult cup moth

The Science Stuff

When it's time for a cup moth caterpillar to become an adult, it spins a hard **cocoon** of silk. The cocoon is attached to a twig.

Inside the cocoon, the caterpillar changes and becomes an adult moth.

The moth emerges from the cocoon by pushing out a tiny, circular cap.

This makes the empty cocoon look like a tiny cup and gives the moth its name.

The Slug Moth Caterpillar

Most caterpillars have six true legs and stubby, leg-like parts called prolegs that help them move. Cup moth caterpillars do not have prolegs.

Instead, these caterpillars produce a silky liquid and use suckers to slide over leaves and twigs. In fact, the way they move is a little like a slug. That's why they are also known as slug moth caterpillars.

UNDERCOVER MOTHS

While some insects warn off or even **repel** their predators, others have **evolved** to simply fade into the background.

During the caterpillar stage of their lives, some looper moths are almost impossible to find on the trees where they feed. Their skin is the color and texture of tree bark. They may even look as if they have patches of lichen, moss, or fungi growing on them. If a predator comes close to one of these little insects, all it sees is a small twig attached to a branch!

Don't Move a Muscle!

To make its twiggy disguise even more realistic, a looper moth caterpillar can stand up straight on its prolegs.

Looper moth caterpillar

Prolegs

The Science Stuff

There are two main ways that insects use shapes and colors to stay hidden from predators: **mimicry** and **camouflage**.

Mimicry

Mimicry is when an insect, or other animal, mimics or looks like something else. For example, a looper moth caterpillar mimics a twig.

Camouflage

Camouflage is when an animal has colors, markings, or a shape that allow it to blend into its background. For example, some adult looper moths have colors and patterns that camouflage them against tree bark or rock.

A looper moth camouflaged on lichen-covered rock

Moving and Measuring

A looper moth caterpillar gets its name from the way in which it moves. It grasps a twig with its six true legs on the front of its body. Then it pulls up its body to form a loop and takes hold of the twig with its rear prolegs. Next, holding on with its prolegs, it reaches out again with its front legs. These caterpillars are sometimes called inchworms because as they move, they look as if they are measuring their journey.

Head

Three pairs of true legs

Loop

Prolegs

Masters of Disguise

Leaf mimic katydids are the insect world's masters of disguise. Sometimes, it's impossible to spot these little creatures until they move their legs or antennae.

These insects don't only mimic perfect green leaves. A leaf mimic katydid may look as if it is covered with fungi or has brown, decaying patches. It might even have rough edges to its wings that make it look like a leaf that has been torn or chewed.

This katydid looks like a ragged leaf with damage to its edges.

Leaf-shaped body

Patch that mimics decay

Head

Most types of leaf mimic katydids live in tropical forests in Central and South America.

Some leaf mimic katydids even look like dead leaves that have fallen to the forest floor.

Antennae

The Science Stuff

No two leaf mimic katydids look exactly the same, even if they are the same **species**. Why?

The main predators of these insects are monkeys, such as tamarins.

A golden lion tamarin eating an insect

If all katydids had the same shape or pattern, smart monkeys would soon learn to spot katydids disguised as leaves. If every katydid is unique, it's much harder for a monkey to figure out what is a real leaf and what is an insect in disguise.

Katy Did, Katy Did!

Katydids get their name because some people think their chirping song sounds as if the insects are saying, "Katy did, Katy did!"

A Double Defense

A tree branch hangs low over a pathway in a forest. The branch is covered with sharp green thorns. Or is it?

The branch's thorny covering is in fact dozens of little insects called thornbugs. To avoid being eaten by bigger insects and other predators, these little bugs mimic thorns.

If a predator discovers the trick, the insect's thorn acts as more than just a disguise. The sharp thorn can be used to give an attacker a vicious and painful jab!

Thornbug

The tough, thorn-like section of the insect's body is called a pronotum. It is part of the insect's exoskeleton.

Nothing to see here . . . just some thorns.

A thornbug is less than half an inch (1 cm) long.

The Science Stuff

A female thornbug lays up to 50 eggs in a slit that she cuts in a branch. She makes the slit with a saw-like body part called an ovipositor.

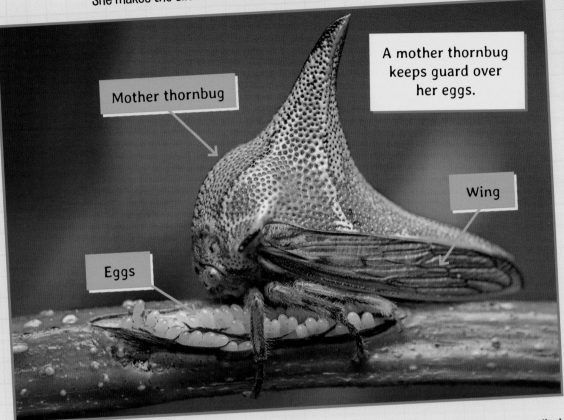

Mother thornbug

A mother thornbug keeps guard over her eggs.

Wing

Eggs

After about 20 days, baby thornbugs, called nymphs, hatch from the eggs.

Now the mother bug must guard her nymphs against wasps and other predators. If a hungry hunter comes close, she stabs at the attacker with her thorn!

Nymphs

Mother thornbug

Protective Shields of Poop

When you're a fat, juicy scarlet lily beetle **larva**, you are in big danger of becoming a bird's dinner. So how do you protect yourself?

Scarlet lily beetle larva

Poop

Once a lily beetle larva hatches from its egg, it starts munching on lily leaves. Soon the larva produces large quantities of poop, which it sticks to its body.

Eating and pooping, the larva quickly builds up a protective shield of poop. Soon the larva looks like a brown, sticky bird dropping.

Now it is safe from hungry predators. After all, nothing wants to eat a lump of bird poop!

Psst! Eric. Is that you in there?

A Good Mom

A female scarlet lily beetle produces plenty of **excrement** and leaves it close to her eggs. Once her larvae hatch, they can use this poop as protection.

The Science Stuff

A Scarlet Lily Beetle's Life Cycle

1 A male and female beetle mate. About two days later, the female lays around 450 orange eggs on the leaves of lily plants.

3 After three weeks, a larva burrows down into the soil. It makes a cocoon with silk from its body. Inside the cocoon, the larva starts to change.

4 After 20 days, the larva emerges as an adult beetle.

Eggs

2 A larva hatches from each egg and feeds on the lilies.

Cocoon

27

Bee-ing a Bee

If it has a fat, furry body with yellow and black stripes, and it's visiting flowers to drink **nectar**, it must be a bumblebee, right? Wrong!

To keep safe from predators, some flies take mimicry to another level. These tricksters fly unharmed around gardens and woodland disguised as a bee or wasp. Birds and other predators avoid eating bees and wasps to keep from getting stung. So some hoverflies, or flower flies, have evolved to mimic their stinging neighbors.

A bumblebee

A hoverfly mimicking a bumblebee

I'm busy as a bee . . . honestly!

Eat Me if You Dare . . .

A hoverfly's yellow and black pattern is a warning sign to predators that it's dangerous. However, the fly can't actually sting an attacker. Predators don't know the fly is harmless, though, and give it a wide berth.

A wasp mimic hoverfly

A wasp

A Big Act

Some hoverflies that mimic wasps pretend they can sting. These tricky customers push the ends of their abdomens into an animal or person's flesh to mimic the action of stinging.

The Science Stuff

How can you tell if an insect is a real bumblebee or a hoverfly in disguise?

Hoverfly

A hoverfly has big eyes that meet or almost meet in the middle.

A hoverfly has short, feathery antennae.

A hoverfly has two wings.

Bumblebee

A bumblebee has long antennae.

A bumblebee has four wings.

A hoverfly has areas on its thorax and abdomen that are not furry.

GLOSSARY

abdomen (AB-duh-muhn)
The rear section of an insect's body that contains its digestive system and reproductive organs.

antennae (an-TEN-ee)
Two long, thin body parts on the head of an insect that it uses for gathering information about its environment.

camouflage (KAM-uh-flahzh)
Colors, markings, or body parts that help an animal blend into its habitat.

cocoon (kuh-KOON)
A case, or covering, made by the larvae of some insects. A larva goes through its pupal life stage and becomes an adult inside its cocoon.

colony (KOL-uh-nee)
A large group of insects that live together and work together to find food, raise young, and protect each other.

echolocation (ek-oh-loh-KAY-shuhn)
A system in which an animal makes a sound that reflects off an object and then returns to the animal's ears. Echolocation is used by some animals to detect and find prey.

evolved (ih-VOLVD)
Developed and changed over a period of time.

excrement (EK-skruh-muhnt)
Another word for poop.

exoskeleton (eks-oh-SKEL-uh-tuhn)
The hard covering that protects the body of an insect.

forage (FOR-ij)
To look for and gather food.

gland (GLAND)
An organ in a person or animal's body that produces chemicals or substances that have a job to do.

larva (LAR-vuh)
The young form of some animals, including insects, fish, and frogs. A caterpillar is a type of larva.

lichen (LYE-kuhn)
A living thing that looks a little like a plant and usually grows on trees or rocks.

mimicry (MIM-ik-ree)
Looking like or acting like another thing.

mite (MITE)
A tiny animal that belongs to the same animal group as spiders and scorpions. Many types of mites live and feed on animals or people.

nectar (NEK-tur)
A sugary liquid produced by flowers.

predator (PRED-uh-tur)
An animal that hunts and eats other animals.

prey (PRAY)
An animal that is hunted by other animals for food.

repel (ri-PEL)
To force or drive something away.

rupture (RUHP-cher)
To break or burst.

species (SPEE-sheez)
Different types of living things. The members of an animal species look alike and can produce young together.

territory (TER-i-tawr-ee)
The area where an animal lives, finds food, and finds mates.

thorax (THAWR-aks)
The middle part of an insect's body between its head and abdomen.

toxic (TOK-sik)
Poisonous.

ultrasonic (uhl-truh-SON-ik)
Sound waves that cannot be detected by human hearing.

venom (VEN-uhm)
Poison that is injected into a person or animal through a bite or sting.

Millions of Insects

Scientists have identified about one million different insect species. There are millions more yet to be discovered, studied, and identified.

INDEX

READ MORE

Owen, Ruth. *Disgusting Animal Defenses (It's A Fact!).* New York: Ruby Tuesday Books (2014).

Wood, Alix. *Amazing Animal Camouflage (Wow! Wildlife).* New York: Rosen Publishing (2013).

LEARN MORE ONLINE

To learn more about insect defenses, go to:
www.rubytuesdaybooks.com/insects